THE
Archive Photographs
SERIES
SALTBURN-BY-THE-SEA

Vans collect and deliver in Saltburn, Redcar, Middlesbro', Stockton Eaglescliffe, The Hartlepools and Surrounding Districts.

⊷ SALTBURN ↶
ELECTRIC LAUNDRY.

Dyeing & Dry Cleaning.

High-class Laundry Work on the Latest and most Improved Methods.

OPEN-AIR DRYING.

The Water at Saltburn-by-the Sea being very soft and clear, the clothes are returned a beautiful colour, without the use of any chemicals whatever.

SPECIALITIES :
Children & Ladies' Finest Work,
Curtains, Flannels.

The Laundry Work for Large Families done quite separately, and on Special Terms.

As there are no Works near it is essentially a Family Laundry.

N.B.—The Saltburn Laundry was the first public Electric Laundry in the kingdom, and has no connection with any other Laundry.

Advertisement for Saltburn Electric Laundry, 1906.

THE
Archive Photographs
SERIES
SALTBURN-BY-THE-SEA

Compiled by
Jean Wiggins

CHALFORD

The Chalford Publishing Company
St Mary's Mill, Chalford,
Stroud, Gloucestershire, GL6 8NX

ISBN 0 7524 1132 2

Typesetting and origination by
The Chalford Publishing Company
Printed in Great Britain by
Bailey Print, Dursley, Gloucestershire

Saltburn Viaduct. A walk through the woods brings the pedestrian close to the site of the former Marske Mill, where the valley is spanned by a red-bricked railway viaduct of eleven arches, each sixty foot high. The railway line is 160 feet above Skelton beck. 'This viaduct jutting into the blue air, with its solid grandeur crossing a valley where tree and shrub forever grow'. Roy A. Rudham, 1996.

Contents

Acknowledgements

May I offer my sincere thanks to Mrs J. Bashford, Mr R. Blacklock, Mrs A. Boagey, Mrs J. Boddy, Mrs B., Mrs A. Collins, Mr E. Crust, Mrs J. Ford, Mr and Mrs T. Gladders, Mr and Mrs A. Gosnay, Miss D. Hinchley, Mrs B. Jones, Mr J.L. King, Mrs P. Lewis, Mrs B. Middleton, Mr N. Noble, Mr and Mrs E. Papprill, Mrs J.G. Pinchin, Mrs A. Pugmire, Mr R.A. Rudham, Mrs J. Scher, Mrs J. Stewart, Mr D. Stewart, Mr A. Stanton, Ollie Smith, Miss J. Taylor, Mr R. Tough, Mrs V. Twidle, Mrs V. Wells, Mrs R. Whitlock and Miss P. Wood. Also to Redcar and Cleveland Museum Services, and Redcar and Cleveland Council. Many thanks also to Pam Wilson who processed the text and to my husband David for his unfailing assistance.

Jean Wiggins, January 1998.

The SS *Ovenbeg* ran aground at Saltburn on 7 May 1924. Her crew abandoned ship when she began to drift dangerously near the pier. Gale force winds and strong waves drove her again and again into the supports of the pier until she, and the pier, was wrecked.

Introduction

Saltburn-by-the-Sea, a name redolent of Victorian grandeur for a spacious, elegant spa resort which, despite times of decay and revival, has retained its unique character and much of its original architecture. What Saltburn is today it owes to its people who are, quite rightly, proud of their heritage. My book explores the heart of Saltburn – the people. When I began my research I did not know what to expect, but I need not have worried. Almost without exception I (a stranger) was welcomed into people's homes to share their memories, and was allowed to use their treasured, irreplaceable photographs. During my research I touched on the lives of residents, past and present, of this delightful resort. The more I learnt the more I realised how little I knew…double enders?…A garden in front of The Ship?…Only one public house inside the town boundary?…Saltburn is a jewel in Cleveland's crown, it has it's own unique character dissimilar to any other town and its beauty provides respite for visitors from surrounding industrial areas. It is vital, in this age of awareness of the need for conservation, that work to repair and restore Saltburn, for future generations, is ongoing. A band of dedicated townspeople are committed to this task. Well done Saltburn!

Britain in Bloom volunteer Brett Thomas.

Three gardeners, thought to be distant relatives of Mr Alan Gosnay. The head gardener, his status declared by his hat, is in the middle. The quality of the photograph reflects its age.

One
Around Saltburn

Sitting pretty, for the camera, is Miss Muriel Hacking.

The Gladders family came to Saltburn from Tyneside in 1864. Thomas Johnson Gladders worked as an engine driver and was involved with the railway for over fifty years. At Loftus, in around 1877, we see him on the footplate of a brand new engine which he was the first person to drive.

Mr Gladders and his wife Eleanor had eleven children, some of whom died in infancy. Over a long period of time the family resided in various houses in Saltburn, also in Loftus, Brotton, Liverton, Guisborough and Redcar. Mr and Mrs Gladders are seen here with their son William James at their home, 2 Zetland Terrace, Saltburn.

The Gladders had four sons, Arthur, Tom, Albert and William James. Arthur was unemployed in 1908 when he found a sovereign while walking on the promenade. He spent the money on cans of milk to sell door to door, found there was a demand and opened a dairy in Milton Street taking his brother William as his partner. This is Arthur aged 28 years.

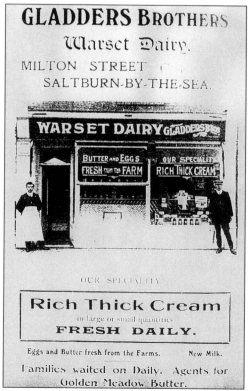

Advertisement for the Gladders Brothers Warset Dairy.

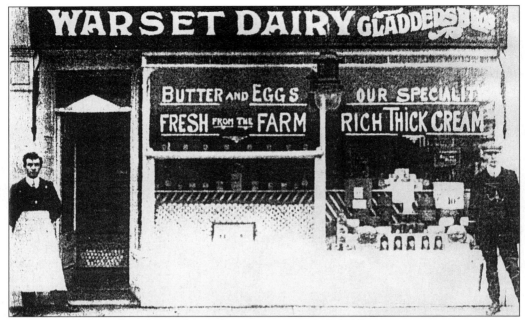

A close up of the Milton Street dairy advertisement, *c.* 1909. William is wearing an apron.

William joined the army in 1914 and later in the war Arthur worked in munitions. Mrs Elizabeth Gladders (William's wife) took over the running of the business, including delivering milk with a pony and trap. This is Elizabeth and William in their garden off Windsor Road in about 1936.

In the early 1920s the business moved to larger premises at 27 Milton Street. Alan (William's son) is shown here wearing his van drivers livery, the year is around 1936. Over the years the dairy had developed into a provisions store. The horse and flat cart which had taken goods out for sale as far as Castleton and Danby, where the driver cried 'eggs, butter and baking powder', and returned to Saltburn with a load of rabbits, hams, cheeses, butter, eggs and poultry bought from farmers, became redundant. In 1935 the first van was purchased, an Austin 10, which was driven by Alan and Hughie (son of Arthur).

William Gladders had trained as a window dresser and often created elaborate displays using crepe paper in the shop windows. William and his family lived above and behind the shop and Elizabeth cooked hams and made potted meat for sale. Ice-cream was also made with cream that arrived, by train from Wiltshire United Dairies, in two gallon cans. Behind the shop was a room with six glass-topped tables where customers could eat their cream ices.

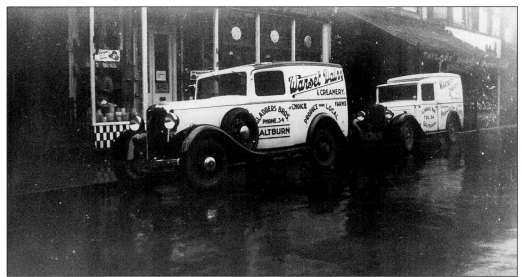

Up to 1936 milk was delivered to the dairy, at the back of the shop, by farmers from Brotton but, after the arrival of the Austin 10 van in 1935 and a second van in 1936, milk was collected from local farms and brought to the dairy.

Tom Gladders (William's son) with the 1936 Bedford van.

VAN WRECKED

A L.N.E.R. passenger train collided with a milk collecting motor-van belonging to Messrs. Gladders Bros. Saltburn, at a level crossing near Brotton about 7.30 a.m., to-day. The driver of the van, Mr. Alan Gladders, aged about 21, son of Mr. W. Gladders, had a remarkable escape.

The engine of the train tore away the rear of the vehicle, and the driver was flung out of the cab, clear of the rails. He received facial cuts and bruises and suffered from shock, but was able to go to his home at Milton-street Saltburn.

MILK ON LINE

The van was wrecked, and the contents of four milk churns was emptied on to the line. Portions of the van were carried some distance along the railway.

Mr. Bottomley, occupier and owner of Shepherd's House Farm, New Brotton, where the milk was collected, saw the accident and hastened to give assistance. On arriving at the scene, he was greatly surprised to find Gladders only slightly hurt.

The train which struck the car was more or less obscured from Gladders' vision by a railway autocar which was travelling in the opposite direction.

It was stated that the crossing gates were open to road traffic at the time of the mishap.

Alan Gladders had some narrow escapes in his van, as this 1935 newspaper cutting illustrates.

In the winter of 1943 Alan and his van were involved in an accident, with a bus, just past Heseltines farm near Brotton. The roads were icy and the van was wrecked but Alan was not hurt. The wrecked van was taken to Princes garage.

With the outbreak of the Second World War Alan became the mainstay of the business. The senior partners, William and Arthur, were still working, they took barrows holding 15 and 17 gallon cans of milk around different areas of Saltburn. The milk was transferred into a two gallon can and measured (1 pint or 1/2 pint) into customers jugs or basins. Rationing and coupons made life more complicated. The business expanded to include supplying school milk and, after the war, a pasteurizing and milk bottling plant were added at the back of the shop. A new grocery shop opened in the 1950s at 100 High Street, Marske. At one time approximately thirty people worked in the business and grocery delivery service. Alan Gladders died in 1965. Hughie, the remaining partner, took over the business, William and Arthur had retired. By 1986 Hughie was ready to retire and the main milk business was sold, the two shops having been sold earlier. Thus ended a family enterprise which was part of the backbone of Saltburn for more than 70 years. Here we see the Gladders family in about 1941, from left to right: Alan, Tom (who later became a poultry farmer and market gardener), William James and son Bill (who had his own milk retail round in East Cleveland).

Mr John Hinchley and his wife Maria Elizabeth of 21 Montrose Street, Saltburn, in 1933. Mr Hinchley worked for Saltburn Urban Council for 36 years. His wife (known as 'nurse' Hinchley) worked for Dr Burnett for over 40 years, delivering babies, attending the sick and dying and laying out the dead. Nurse Hinchley was often paid in kind for her services - eggs, fish, sometimes bits of furniture, whatever people had to give her. She was very well respected in the community.

Nurse Hinchley's daughter Frances Amy, born 1904, accompanied her mother from an early age to learn her trade, then worked with her mother before carrying on the family tradition herself. In addition to her mothers duties Frances took over mortuary work – the laying out, washing and tidying of bodies which came into the mortuary near the Ship Inn from shipwrecks. Neither she nor her mother had any professional qualifications but were always ready to help in an emergency. This unusual photograph shows Frances Hinchley aged 17 with her nephew William.

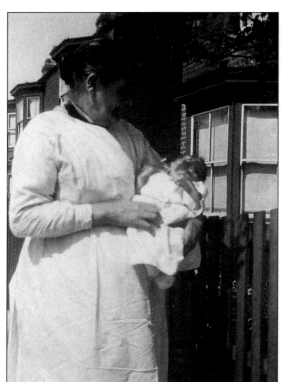

Maria Hinchley with a family baby,
outside 21 Montrose Street.

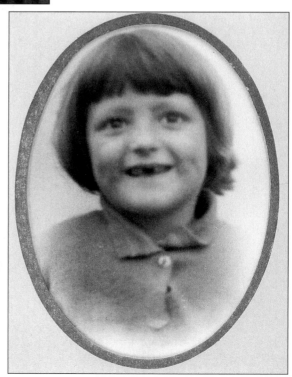

Miss Dora Hinchley aged 5 in a school
photograph from May 1933.

Albert Rudham aged 14 is on the front row, third from left. This group of boys were employed by the railway at Saltburn as engine cleaners in 1911. Albert later became a fireman and then an engine driver.

Mr Albert Rudham, engine driver for British Rail, in 1954. Mr Rudham lived in Oxford Street, Saltburn.

John William 'Jack' Gosnay from Sheffield married Hetty Wade of Stockton in 1923. The couple came to Saltburn when Jack took employment with Mr Birdsall, butcher, of Milton Street. Hetty and Jack lived in Eden Street. When Mr Birdsall became ill in 1927 and moved to the South of England the business (butcher's and three shops on the same block and a slaughterhouse and premises leased to Redcar Gas Company) went up for auction at the Zetland Hotel. Jack (an entrepreneur of his time) found some backers and bought the lot, moving his wife and family into rooms over the shop. Hetty and Jack Gosnay are seen here on their wedding day.

In the early 1930s Jack bought the fever hospital and turned the wards into battery hen houses, bringing relatives from Sheffield to run the chicken farm. Jack sold meat on the bone - full briskets and sirloins. The Jewel Streets had lots of boarding houses so business was brisk. Jack would go to Guisborough or Stokesley cattle mart and employ a drover to walk his beasts back to Saltburn to graze on fields in the area of the (now) caravan site. Derrick Gosnay is shown feeding beasts. Saltburn is in the background.

Harry Hoggett outside Gosnays butchers, c. 1937. Jack took down the glass canopy over the shops in the 1930s. When needed the beasts were brought to the 'hunger room' where they had water but no food for twenty four hours before they were slaughtered. Children would haul on a bull rope to pull a cow down to the ground before it was shot. They were then given the cow's bladder to dry, blow up, and use as a football.

Gosnays shop. During the war Hetty lost all the men from the shop to conscription, so she leased the premises to Dewhirsts until 1965 when her son Alan took over.

An early Victorian Week photograph of Gary Roper, Michael Gosnay and father Alan, in the shop.

The first school preaching room in Saltburn. Perhaps this building was originally an engine house or a platelayers cabin.

The Valley Gardens and bridge, with fairy lights on the bandstand, *c.* 1906.

Saltburn Italian Gardens in the 1930s or 1940s.

Mr Alf King of Saltburn. When you look at Mr John King you see a successful businessman, but it was not always so. John's father, Alf King (a newsagent, stationer and tobacconist in Saltburn since around 1957), was a gentleman of military bearing who died suddenly in 1971 unexpectedly leaving two shops (in Dundas Street and Station Street) to John. Until then John had spent most of his life in the countryside, working as a cattle buyer. To move from the Midlands with his wife, Prue, and children at a comparatively young age was a big decision to make. John and his family travelled north in a horse box with some furniture, Prue's horse and £25 to take over a business which was completely foreign to them.

John King in his office. The shop in Station Street had long mahogany counters holding piles of magazines and newspapers and sweet and cigarette sections, with books at the rear. Upstairs to the right was china (mainly dinner ware and cut glass), toys were on the left. At first John had to rely on staff for advice and guidance. Later John acquired Mrs Laverick's sweet and tobacco shop, (also in Station Street), to which the china and glass were transferred as a separate unit. The Dundas Street shop was sold and the Station Street newsagent's shop was further enlarged to offer a wider and more varied selection of goods. To accommodate an increasing demand for outdoor toys the showroom was extended into part of the old post office, next door. Now, 26 years after John took up his father's challenge, glass, china and fancy goods in great variety are for sale once again in the main shop which is probably at least four times larger than in Alf King's day. Over the years John has become a specialist in his field. His father would be proud of him. John says, 'Saltburn is like a magnet to people who live here - if you have to leave it, it always draws you back, it is a very friendly town.' Also, 'If you treat people with dignity and respect, generations of customers return.'

J. Wedgwood

Tobacconist, Newsagent, Stationer & Fancy Dealer——

22, MILTON STREET,
14, STATION STREET,
SALTBURN-BY-THE-SEA.

Advertisement for J. Wedgewood, 1906. This tobacconist and newsagent was, in later years, taken over by Alf King.

Mr 'Clarrie' Stewart founded Consteel (concrete and steel) Technical Services at Saltburn, in the former Electricity Board showroom, on the corner of Bath Street during the summer of 1976. Clarrie had worked as a draughtsman in industry for many years and had become increasingly frustrated by lengthy procedures and red tape. Now he was able to work in his own innovative way. Together with his son Derrick and Ross, an old colleague, a new way of working was developed. Going it alone was a gamble which soon became a success. More staff were recruited and a branch at South Bank was later added. Work came in from around the world. Now Derrick is in charge and employs around forty local draughtsmen and engineers at Consteel - a fitting memorial to Clarrie.

For many years Ted Papprill, a dental technician, cherished an ambition to build and own a pub. Ted and his wife Terry were involved in the running of the Middle House, Marske with Terry's parents for twenty years, then spent ten years as licensees of the pub, finishing in 1980. Ted's solicitor Peter Nixon knew of premises in Dundas Street, Saltburn, which had once been the business of Mr W. Rapp, stationer and printer, and were now standing empty. Ted's plans for alterations passed the planning inquiry, and he was granted a licence for the premises - with the proviso that he cleared a covenant applied by the Quaker Founding Fathers of Saltburn in 1862. The Quakers, from Darlington, had imposed a ban on public houses and other trades including soap boiling, candle making, and fell mongering (dealing in animal skins). Saltburn has three Hotels with public bars which are not covered by the prohibition, but the only pub, The Ship, is outside the town boundaries. It was two years after Ted first drew up the plans for his Victorian-style pub before Ted and Terry won their bitter £100,000 anti-prohibition battle at a Lands Tribunal in Durham. Peter and Tony Nixon worked very hard to get the covenant removed. Ted and Terry lived in a caravan at Tockett's Mill for eighteen months awaiting the realisation of Ted's dream. The bitter wrangles for and against the pub were very stressful, but eventually the covenant was broken and Ted employed contractors and worked alongside them to build his pub. The Victoria opened with a celebration on 7 December 1982. Here we see Ted behind the bar.

W. Rapp and Sons, booksellers and lenders, stationers, printers and house and estate agents of Dundas Street, Saltburn. Mr Rapp is pictured outside his shop in around 1906.

Terry in Victorian costume. Ted revelled in his role as landlord. Terry was cook and their two daughters, son and daughter-in-law worked with them, together with twelve other members of staff. The pub was a hit from the start and later it was further extended to take in the corner shop. Lunches and evening meals were served and the function room upstairs was open until two in the morning. Terry catered for the Round Table, Sports Club, Ladies Luncheon Club, The Jazz Club and many more organizations, and still maintained high standards with bar meals and in the general running of the pub. Ted and Terry found their new life exhilarating and creative, but rarely found any time for themselves.

The Victoria, Saltburn. In 1986 Terry suffered a stroke and a heart attack on the same day, attributed to stress, and was ill again a year later. Ted knew it was time to leave. The Victoria was sold to Mr Ian Smith. In January 1990 Terry and Ted moved to Marske. Ted has no regrets about leaving, he achieved his ambition. Terry says 'I helped Ted because I love him'.

The Queen Hotel, 1906.

A confirmation procession from Our Lady of Lourdes church, Saltburn 1936.

The procession winds its way alongside the railway embankment in 1936.

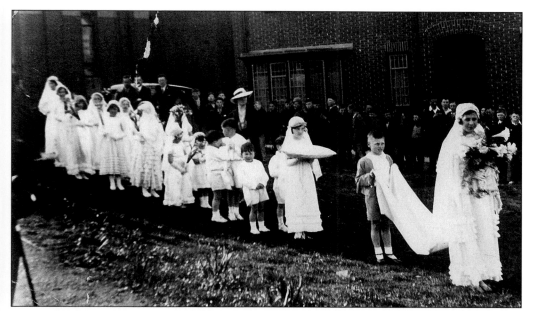

A close up of the children in this 1936 confirmation procession through Saltburn.

Dorothy and Lena Sanders, by Pitchforth
of Milton Street, Saltburn.

In the 1930s Mr Hill opened his first greengrocers and florists shop in Milton Street. Reilly's the optician's stands on this spot today. Mr Hill kept a market garden in Saltburn Lane opposite Rushpool Hall. His family later bought a garden in Stokesley which remains today.

Teddy's Nook. Built by Henry Pease, for his own habitation, this sturdy sandstone house was first named The Cottage. The following stories (whether fact or fiction is not known) all relate to this house. When Saltburn Bank was only a track, two eccentric ladies, who lived in the house, kept a lion for a pet. They exercised it on the beach daily and it is said to be buried somewhere in the garden. Mrs Lillie Langtry (the Jersey Lily) stayed at the house at sometime between 1877 and 1880. She was often visited by Edward, Prince of Wales (later Edward V11) who had a suite of rooms at the Zetland Hotel. The Cottage, consequently, became known as Teddy's Nook. In wartime German spies are thought to have contacted ships out at sea by means of flashing lights from Teddy's Nook. The Kelly family, who leased the house in later years, were cousins of Jimmy Saville who visited regularly.

The Zetland Hotel, Saltburn, 1906.

Mrs Audrey Collins had lived in Saltburn for fifteen years when she was invited by Mr Edwin Schofield to join Saltburn and Marske District Council in 1967. Mrs Collins had no previous experience of local government work but, the following year, she became chairman of Foreshore and Gardens, a post that she loved. Saltburn and Marske Council had been in existence since 1894 and became a joint authority with Marske in 1932. From 1972 to 1973 Mrs Collins was Mayor of the Council, shortly before Cleveland County came into being. Saltburn and Marske were to be swallowed up by Langbaurgh District with an estimated population of 140,000 and a rateable value of £8.5 million pounds.

Audrey Collins was well aware that once Saltburn was part of the larger authority money would be diverted, by the Labour Council, into poorer areas, for which she was deeply concerned, whereas Saltburn, which was considered a middle class area needing nothing, would get very little. During her year in office Audrey saw the building of the much fought for, £374,000, Sports Complex get under way, and preparation beginning for the opening of the new Baths. A measure of agreement had been reached with British Rail about re-siting the station and the release of the excursion line - both necessary in order to re-develop the derelict station site which divided the town. Here we see Councillor Collins, Clerk to the Council Mr Morgan (left) and architect Mr A. Mallory. The latter presented Mrs Collins with a spade, to cut the first sod for Saltburn's Sports Complex, on 4 October 1972.

Audrey Collins made, in vain, a last ditch attempt in 1974 to convince Langbaurgh and Cleveland Councils that, after over a hundred years of collapses, re-building, constant repairs and neglect, Saltburn Pier must be saved. The Councils set aside £30,000 for work on the pier which was declared unsafe in 1973, had since lost five of its legs, and was at constant risk of storm damage. It was proposed and agreed that if no grant was forthcoming the pier would be demolished. Audrey launched a bitter attack on the council's Labour group, 'They never had the slightest intention of saving it, but I'm not going to sit back and see the pier demolished and I don't think the people of Saltburn will, either!' Mrs Collins said she would personally lead a public appeal for funds to save the pier if no money would be granted by official sources.

After a bitter wrangle and a public inquiry it was decided that the pier would live again in a shortened form costing an eventual £113,000 to renovate. An attempt to stop the scheme was defeated 30 to 22 on a recorded vote. One councillor said he could find no enthusiasm, from the people in his ward, for this 'great rusty dagger sticking in the side of Langbaurgh'. Saltburn had lost a lot of its heritage, the Ha'penny Bridge (the saving of which had also been vigorously campaigned for by Mrs Collins) had been blown up and the Zetland Hotel and Railway Station were under threat. It was alleged that the Labour group had committed themselves to the destruction of the bridge and pier while still in Saltburn and Marske Council.

Saltburn, a planner's dream in the nineteenth century was now crumbling away. The victory over the fate of the pier took on a deeper significance and was the catalyst for the beginning of a campaign to restore Saltburn to some of its former glory. Councillor Audrey Collins is pictured with Councillor Douglas Moore at the reopening of the pier on 29 July 1978.

Councillor Audrey Collins, at the sink, doing her regular, monthly, voluntary stint helping to prepare meals for the elderly at Saltburn WRVS centre.

Audrey Collins – your Conservative candidate. At Overdene, medical and logistical reasons were used to justify the closure of Saltburn's Maternity Home, which Audrey Collins fought to protect. Forty two campaigners travelled to the House of Commons to meet Health Minister Dr Gerard Vaughn, who intervened to win a reprieve for the unit a week before it was due to close. When he travelled up to see the hospital however, he found that the Area Health Authority had removed all the equipment before he arrived to discuss the review, thus forcing the hospital's closure. Mrs Collins left Saltburn after her husband's death in 1986 but stayed involved with the council until the next election, at which point she stood down. After leaving Saltburn she continued her long standing work for the South Tees Health Authority and finally retired in November 1997 after 37 years with the hospital services. Audrey Collins remembers her time in Saltburn with affection and feels very privileged to have lived and worked there.

I met Jackie Taylor for the first time on 4 November 1997 and discovered that this warm, welcoming, modest lady is single-minded in her desire to see Saltburn restored to some of its former glory. Jackie moved to Saltburn in 1987 to be near her family, she was overwhelmed by the kindness of local people and determined to do something in return for the town she loves.

After joining the Residents Association she initiated a scheme to decorate the town centre with lights at Christmas. Audrey Boagey, Carol Miller, Veronica Bowland and Jackie called on every shopkeeper to gauge their opinions and soon everyone wanted to join in. Jackie was a Nursing Officer at West Suffolk Hospital and had once raised money for a hospital swimming pool, so she was a good organiser. She asked the Residents Association if she could start a fund raising arm within the Association. She called it the 500 Club, five being Jackie's lucky number and 500, the number of members she hoped to attract.

The 500 Club became independent in 1990, its aims are to preserve and enhance the beauty of Saltburn. There are now well over 500 members who pay £1 per month subscription. Often working in conjunction with other groups, the 500 club maintains and places seats around the town, looks after and replaces litter bins, refurbishes street name signs, maintains the town centre gardens, encourages waste re-cycling and litter picking and fund raises endlessly. Jackie calls on a band of people affectionately known as Jackie's Army for help with her endeavours. Winning Northumbria in Bloom in 1988, Best Small Town in 1991 and other awards sparked off much enthusiasm. Jackie can be seen here at the recent opening ceremony of a new bandstand (front row left).

Jackie with Peter Fenton at the new bandstand. The £100,000 bandstand was opened, on Thursday 24 July 1997, by the Mayor of Redcar and Cleveland Borough Council with the first concert given by Marske Band. The opening celebrated a six-year dream come true for Jackie Taylor and Peter Fenton, architect, who donated his services to the project. Jackie and the 500 Club raised £20,000 of the total and Jackie received £63,500, in 1996, from the Arts Lottery Fund. This, with other grants and contributions, made up the full amount.

Marske Band play the opening concert, 24 July 1997. The 500 Club project is still ongoing. Vandal screens are needed and more permanent seating, funds are also required to pay the bands who give concerts. The 500 Club is also involved in a project to get disabled access to the beach at Hazel Grove, in partnership with other groups. What comes next I wonder? Jackie Taylor brings out the best in people and, undoubtably, is the driving force behind the 500 Club.

Jackie Taylor's home in Cleveland Street, Saltburn, 1997.

A flower-filled boat in Marske Lane, Saltburn, 1997.

Santa and his elves arrive in Saltburn, Christmas 1996.

Santa's Grotto. The children of Saltburn always enjoy Santa's visits.

Two
Beside the Sea

Alan Gosnay and cousin Freda on
the beach at Saltburn, 1925.

Post-war Huntcliff and the Ship Inn. Certain rocks in the direction of Huntcliff were left bare at low tide where 'Seales in greate heardes like swine' were seen to be basking in the sun. 'For their better scuritye', says the medieval writer, 'They put in use a kind of military discipline, warily preparing against a soddaine surprize, for on the outermost rocke one great seale or more keeps sentinell, which upon the first inklinge of any danger, giveth the alarme to the rest by throweing of stones, or making a noise in the water, when he tumbles down from the rocke the rest immediately doe the like, insomuch that yt is very hard to overtake them by cunning.' This quotation comes from the Cottonian manuscript.

East Beach, Saltburn-by-the-Sea. 15421.

I do like to be beside the seaside - Saltburn east beach prior to the Second World War.

These lovely children are dressed for an outing, sadly their names are not known.

Mr John Cook with Barrie and niece Pauline at the beach amusements, Saltburn, *c*. 1955.

On the beach, 1931. Great grandma Hinchley with baby Fred, Nora Omerod, Dora Hinchley (in a white dress), Amy Swift, Jack Pugmire, and Frances Amy Pugmire with a child on her knee.

Derrick, or Alan, Gosnay with *Ella* the dog, at Saltburn, 1929.

Derrick, *Ella*, and Alan Gosnay at Saltburn.

Derrick or Alan Gosnay.

Grandma Gosnay and Derrick, at Saltburn.

Mr Alan Stanton, foundryman and part-time fisherman, in 1938, aged 26 years. Alan fished for his hobby. Most fishing boats at Saltburn were double enders rather than Yorkshire cobles. Cobles were difficult to manoeuvre while setting sail or coming ashore at Saltburn, when their sole method of propulsion was oars. Fish were so plentiful that no one could make a living out of selling them, most people fished for themselves. Whiting and codling were caught beyond the pier. During the depression in the 1930s there were gluts of fish - a hundred mackerel could be caught in a couple of hours and sold at one dozen for 4d, and a 5lb cod was 6d.

Here we see Alan Stanton beaching one of his double ender fishing boats. Please note the bandstand and shelters on the end of the pier.

Alan and his sister Mary on the beach at Saltburn, they were caught on camera by Cyril Wardle in the summer of 1939.

Mr Stanton obtained a licence enabling him to carry twelve passengers on pleasure trips along the coast. He charged 6d for adults and 3d for children. In the late 1930s he took holidaymakers out to see the minesweeper HMS *Saltburn*. Alan has his hand on the tiller as he guides his boat ashore.

Cranking up old *Reliance*, one of Alan Stanton's boats, on a pleasure trip. It is possible to see on this photograph that double enders have two bows and no flat stern like cobles, which are more suited to small bays like Runswick Bay and Staithes. Alan's boat is seen here, at the bottom of the picture, in 1938.

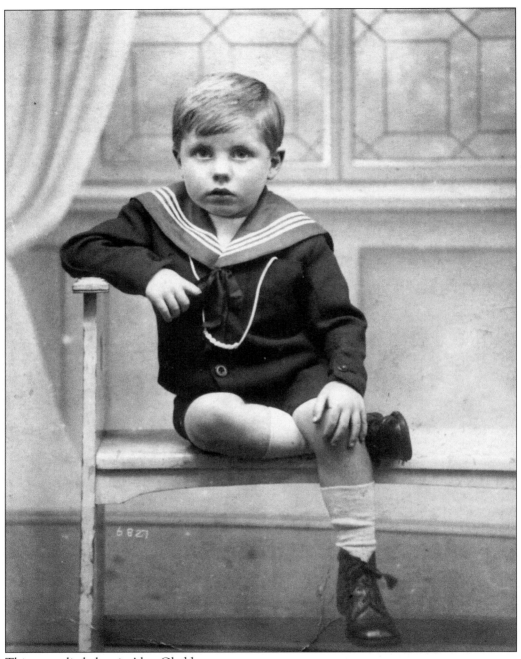

This smart little boy is Alan Gladders.

Saltburn Miniature Railway. The original line, built by Mr H. Dunn of Bishop Auckland, was approximately 300 yards long. It ran from a point on the beck side of the path to the Valley Gardens, almost opposite the old Brine Baths Pump House, through a tunnel and along the flood plain of the beck at the foot of the steep hillside. The line was single throughout, there being no turnouts or points. Herbert Dunn opened the line in 1947 and acquired a Parkinson petrol locomotive, for which he doubled the length of the line, in 1948. This early sepia postcard shows the line. Pay at the shed for the railway and Valley Gardens, come out through the turnstile. Just visible in the background is Dove's caravan site.

In 1949 Mr Dunn obtained a unique miniature steam locomotive, the 1909 *Blacolvesley* later named *Elizabeth*.

Postcard of Lakeside Miniature Railway, Saltburn, *c.* 1953. In 1950 the line was sold to Councillor J.C. Pickering and extended to its present length. In 1953 a new electric locomotive, *Prince Charles*, arrived. For a couple of seasons *Prince Charles* and *Elizabeth* worked together, mainly at peak periods. To facilitate this a siding was put in near the present northern terminus. *Elizabeth* was sold in 1968 and, after Mr Pickering retired in 1974, the railway was sold to Cleveland Transit. However, a landslide and other difficulties meant that the line had to be put out to contract. Although taken over by dedicated enthusiast, Mr Brian Leonard, the railway was impossible to revive.

The *Prince Charles* with (left to right) Colin Gatenby, Ray Ireland, Reg Blacklock and George Althwaite in 1992. The line lay derelict until 1983 when Mr Arthur Ling, in an attempt to revive the railway, called a public meeting at Saltburn from which the Saltburn Miniature Railway Association was born. The intention of the association was to raise money to reopen the railway. While fund raising, volunteers began the onerous task of restoring the track, engine and rolling stock.

George Althwaite, one of a band of sterling volunteers, had this red and black, diesel hydraulic locomotive named after him. This engine was built by volunteers at Saltburn.

Little Imp. This 1905 steam locomotive, owned by John Henderson of Northallerton, visited Saltburn between 1996 and 1997. Saltburn Miniature Railway has only twelve volunteers - more may be needed. There has never been a female train driver, perhaps some intrepid lady might like to volunteer!

Surfing with boards began at Saltburn in the mid 1960s with a few dedicated enthusiasts including Tim Gladders, John Roughton, John Smith and Ian Davies, who quickly developed their own scene and hung out together. Ian and John Roughton opened a surf shop in Emerald Street a few years later, making boards and selling equipment, but it closed after a couple of years. Nick Noble started surfing in the 1970s when it was still rare to see surfing in this country. Surfers came to Saltburn from Manchester, Leeds and all over the north of England to enjoy their sport. Saltburn lends itself to those just learning to surf. The gentle, sloping beach, which faces north and is open to a long area of sea, gets good waves and swell which travels between Teesmouth and Whitby from the Arctic. In 1983 Nick set up an equipment hire business, trading from the back of a van. He started with a handful of surfboards, a couple of wet suits and a few windsurfers which he had hired and slowly added to his stock. At that time the season would end in September but better suits, boots and gloves meant that surfing gradually became a year round sport. Later Nick, and friend Gary, opened the Surf Shop on the lower promenade. Nick (left) and Gary are here outside their shop, sometime in 1996 or 1997.

Surfer Chris Erie can barely be seen under the curl of a wave off Saltburn. Surfers vigorously campaign against pollution. Unfortunately, waste of all kinds is dumped in the sea. Over the last seven years Surfers Against Sewage, which began in Cornwall and has become nationwide with a powerful 20,000 lobby, has become very influential. Biological treatment is needed, but is not forthcoming, for sewage, to eliminate the viruses which can cause many illnesses, some severe, to all who enjoy the sea. Hopefully, new pollution laws may soon come from Europe which will end our antiquated system, which causes distress to people and wildlife alike.

Nick Noble surfs in the Autumn Surfing Contest, 1996. From their surf shop Nick and Gary organize surf contests accompanied by social events. They also run a Sunday League for young aspiring (competitive) surfers. People involve themselves physically and mentally with this sport and there is great camaraderie among them. While enjoying themselves they are also gaining an awareness and respect for the environment they are using. While surfing, seals can often be seen as well as fish jumping out of the sea, cormorants, and the occasional porpoise and basking shark. People of all ages are happy together, 'surfing is a great leveller', says Nick. And the future? Surfing at Saltburn goes from strength to strength and is becoming a major asset to the town, perhaps someone might consider providing a warm changing room on the lower promenade for the growing band of people who suffer year round discomfort to follow their sport.

Three
Wartime

In 1914 James Gladders joined the Royal
Artillery, he is on the right of this
photograph.

A First World War Howitzer gun.

The Howitzer gun in Flanders with its crew of seven and a dog found along the way. William Gladders worked on this gun though it is not known if he is on this photograph. At one point in the war the gun received a direct hit and William was the sole survivor.

William, here with other soldiers, having a rest at the YMCA. He is at the right end of the middle row.

First World War soldiers, on their way to the front, have a send off parade at the old school, Marske Road, Saltburn. 'They gave their lives, to live in our hearts, until we meet again'. Roy A. Rudham, 1996.

Stand at ease. Jack Pugmire is on the left.

Saltburn-by-the-Sea Home Guard, on the Bottom Promenade, in 1943. Albert Rudham is fifth from right on the front row.

Joseph Rudham (1920-1995) here in Montreal, Canada, in 1943. He left school aged 14 and worked at Smith's Dock as an apprentice Marine Engineer. He was retained at the dock during 1939-42, as his was a reserve occupation, but in 1942 he volunteered to join the Merchant Navy where he served as 5th Engineering Officer for the rest of the war. He was awarded the Atlantic and Italy Stars, the 1939-45 Star and the 1939-45 Service Medal.

Miss Vera Craggs of Wheatley Hill, County Durham (now Mrs Vera Wells of Saltburn). Here she is the Carnival Queen of Cullingworth, near Bradford, in 1940.

Vera Craggs was only seventeen when she joined the ATS in 1941. Wanting to escape from a boring job she gave a false age of eighteen when she joined up and, when she was asked what career she had chosen she said 'cook', copying the girl in front of her. Vera was sent to the Duke of Wellington`s Barracks in Halifax. She was trained by men and with men, including parades and drills, for six weeks. Next she was transferred to Luton Hoo - a stately home which was headquarters for Eastern Command Home Forces and where security was very tight. After spending three months in damp and draughty barracks she was taken ill and later transferred to Saltburn, where she was billeted at Norwood House. Vera cooked and worked in the dining rooms of the Royal Army Ordnance Corps, for clerks and storemen who were training at Saltburn. There were four dining rooms, the Parochial Hall, Overdene, Riftswood Hall and the former Theatre (now the saleroom). Men were billeted in commandeered houses and the Zetland Hotel. The Officers Mess, where the officers ate and slept, was at Manesty. Here we see a shift of cooks and boilermen outside the theatre building.

Vera's shift in 1943 - Jean Glover, Olive Dunn, Chris Macdonald, May Bankhurst, Pat Hay, Vera Craggs (second from right, front row), Dot Wilson, Corporal Flarerly, Madge Booth and Dot Campbell.

W/82228 Private Vera Craggs, aged 19, is wearing her Glengarry or forage cap in this stunning photograph taken, during her tea break, by Forrest Wompra of Milton Street in 1943. Mr Alf Hodgson introduced Vera to Mr Joe Rudham whom she later married. Vera has spent most of her life in Saltburn.

Sergeant Betty Seaton (Vera's friend) at Saltburn, 1942. The NAAFI was in the Zetland Hotel, an army band played for dances at the Spa and the WVS, in Ruby Street, served hot food and put on concerts for service personnel. In the summer of 1944 a bomb dropped on Overdene Lodge and it was rumoured that a young soldier was killed when a wall fell on him.

Platoon photograph - Company C of RAOC. Sergeant Massingham of Saltburn is on the third row, sixth from the right. Redcar girl Margaret Robinson is on the top row, left end, and Vera Craggs is on the fourth row, eighth from the right. The platoon posed on the lawn at Brockley House, Saltburn in 1942.

Miss Joan Massender (Mrs Joan Ford of Saltburn) wrote to the Admiralty to ask to join the WRNS, with her friend Rita, when she was called up in 1942. She was offered, and accepted, a job as pay writer and was sent to college in London for one month to learn about Naval pay. Naval book keeping was started by Samuel Pepys and, apart from the use of quill pens, it has remained the same. Joan was posted to Chatham where she worked on prisoner of war pay to men in German POW camps. This is Joan at Chatham in 1942.

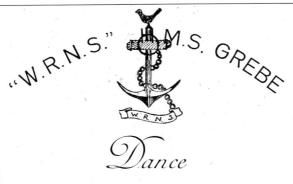

"W.R.N.S." H.M.S. GREBE

Dance

(By Kind Permission of Comder H. R. B. HOWELL, R. N.
COMMANDING OFFICER H. M. S. GREBE)

WILL BE HELD AT THE

ALEXANDRIA FLEET CLUB

ON

THURSDAY 20TH JULY 1944

7,30 - 11,30

Dance card, July 1944. After volunteering to go abroad Joan was sent to Egypt on the troop ship *Orion*. The ship was bombed by German planes in the Mediterranean but no one was hurt. The destroyer *Sheffield* which was part of the *Orion's* escort was torpedoed. Joan arrived in Alexandria on Christmas Eve 1943 and was billeted in an elegant French house. She was put in charge (Leading Wren) of pay for all the small ships - destroyers, corvettes and the like, in the Mediterranean. The Eighth Army (Desert Rats) were in Tobruck, fighting was spasmodic but there was no trouble in Alexandria. Lots of dances and social occasions were held at the Fleet Club and attended by Wrens, sailors from port and on leave, and members of the RAF. There were also cinemas showing American films.

Joan visiting the pyramids, Cairo, in 1944. The Egyptians seemed to be very anti-British. Perhaps they felt that we had dragged them into the war because of the need to protect the Suez Canal.

Joan and friends on Aboukir beach,
Christmas Eve, 1944.

Flight docket, 1944.

NAME L/WREN MASSENDER "PRIORITY" Nil   Serial No. _____

ACCOMMODATION HAS BEEN RESERVED ON   RAF   PLANE.   R. T. O.

FROM WILHELMA TO CAIRO ON 14/8/44   14 AUG. 1944

Returning from _____ TO _____ ON _____   CAIRO MAIN

Note: Passengers who have booked return accommodation must
arrival to Movements 8 (AIR) G.H.Q. M.E.F. otherwise such return
booking will not be reserved after midday, day previous scheduled
departure.

You should report at   0830   hrs L.T. at AIR MOVTS WILHELMA

LUGGAGE ALLOWANCE   40   lbs.

CAR LEAVES KING DAVID HOTEL ANNEX, JERUSALEM AT _____ hrs L.T.

PLANE LEAVES   0900   hrs L.T. from   WILHELMA

AUTHORITY FOR PASSAGE MOV & TN, LEVANT AREA, TEL 4651 EXT 134 & 97

SECURITY CONTROL
1 4 AUG. 1944
R.A.F. Station, LYDDA.

FOR COLONEL,
D.D.MOV.

Sailing on the Nile, Luxor 1945.

When war in Europe finished a victory parade was held in the Stadium, Alexandria, June 1945.

V-J DAY

H.M.S. VALLURU   AUGUST 15TH 1945

VJ day parade at HMS *Valluru*, 1945. Most Wrens were sent to Malta and Gibralta on their way home. Joan had asked to be allowed to join her fiancé, civilian engineer Harold Ford in India. She travelled on a troop ship from Aden to Bombay - the only woman on board. From Bombay she was sent to Ceylon to work on Fleet Air Arm Station Valluru near Madras.

Wrens in the Victory March Past, August 1945. Joan Massender is in the fourth row, second from the left.

Joan and her friends on her wedding day. Harold Ford and Joan Massender were married in Madras Cathedral on 4 December 1945. After a ten day honeymoon Joan returned to her base to find the Navy gone and the RAF in charge. Her Commander-in-Chief in Ceylon gave her permission to discharge, to the delight of her husband who took her home with him to Calcutta.

Miss H (who prefers to remain anonymous) joined one of the first ATS units in June 1939. Her commander was a very wealthy woman who watched her girls drill for the first time wearing a brightly coloured feather hat, a mink coat and high-heeled shoes. Miss H got her first posting to Erith opposite Tilbury docks. Her unit had no uniforms, they still wore civvy clothes. The docks were bombed almost every night for six months, the girls were very brave.

Miss H was promoted to Corporal and had eight girls in her intake. As the ATS was in its infancy rules were made up as the women went along and sometimes things got chaotic. With the onset of war uniforms and kitbags were issued. Corporal H worked as secretary to the Adjutant. One day, observing her coming up some steps, he asked what was wrong with her knee – embarrassingly her army issue lock-knit bloomer leg had slipped way below her skirt!

Some of the male forces were hostile at having to work with women. However, Corporal H made her girls indispensable and she and her ladies were sent a bouquet of carnations by their Colonel. Corporal H became Subaltern and was posted to Hereford to a Driver Training section. She learnt to drive 3 ton lorries then taught her platoon, taking learner drivers out in lorries, in the Welsh mountains, in the middle of winter. Here we see Subaltern H taking the salute (back to the camera) at Hereford.

Officer H, on the right, 1943. Later Subaltern H became Company Commander at Wakefield. She met her future husband during the last six months of the war, Army Lieutenant B who came from Durham. After the war Mr and Mrs B lived in Brancepeth, in County Durham, before moving to Saltburn. Mrs B loved life in the army and tackled everything that came along. The role of women in the Forces must never be under estimated.

Miss Joan Indge (Mrs Joan Pinchin of Saltburn) lived in Upminster, Essex, when she joined the ATS in June 1942. After one month of initial training as a teleprinter in Dalkeith she was posted to Fulford Barracks, York. Sadly she was not happy there, so decided to re-muster (change her job) and was sent to offices in Leeds, which had been taken over by the Army, where she became Sergeant Indge, in charge of the orderly room. Joan was attached to the Royal Corps of Signals and girls on charges, from barracks all around the area, were sent to her office. Here we see the Sergeants Mess, Wetherby Road, Leeds with Joan in the centre of the back row in 1944.

Wedding photograph of Corporal Pinchin and Segeant Indge. While still in Upminster Joan became the pen friend of RAF Corporal Leslie Pinchin of Redcar, who had joined up in 1939. Their first meeting was under the clock at Waterloo Station in September 1942 and they were married in 1943.

Sergeant Joan Pinchin (second from right) and friends, March 1945.

Leslie Pinchin (second from left, front row) playing the saxaphone in an RAF and Italian prisoner of war dance band, Algiers 1944. Two weeks after the wedding of Joan and Leslie Pinchin, Leslie was re-located from Bournemouth to Algiers. While on board the *Windsor Castle*, and waiting to dock, his ship was torpedoed by an Italian submarine, with great loss of life. Leslie jumped into the sea and was saved. He came home, in 1946, to his parent's house in Redcar, where Joan was waiting for him.

Four
Sport and Leisure

First Saltburn Girl Guides Camp,
Ruswarp, 1924.

Saltburn Council Football Club. Stanley Hinchley, aged 19, is behind the boy with the football.

We see here the new swimming baths car park, in Marske Mill Lane, where football matches were played. Ronnie Hinchley is second from left on the back row.

Saltburn 1st Congregational Football Team, 1936. Back row, from left to right: Messrs J. Stanton (secretary), A. Ward (trainer), H. Evans, J. Theaker, A. Coates, F. Sutton, R. Cook, G. Watson, M. Jones and J. Fenny. Front row, from left to right: B. Stanton, A. Russell, H. Elliot, R. Batty and H. Johnson.

Saltburn Rover Scouts, c. 1930.

Saltburn Church Lads Brigade Band, outside Ebenezer church.

Members of Saltburn Church Lads Brigade, camping at Bridlington, *c.* 1936.

Saltburn-by-the-Sea Brine Baths.

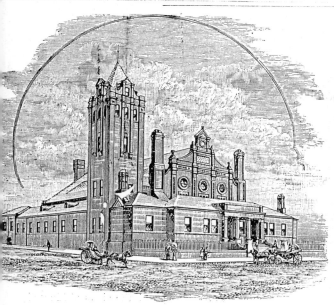

THESE BATHS, which are situated close to the Railway have been erected specially for the Brine Treatme[n] has been found so efficacious in the cure of Rheumati[s] Lumbago, Sciatica, Neuralgia, Rheumatic Gout, Para at similar establishments in the West of England. The brought from Salt Wells in the neighbourhood, and is TEN SALT AS ORDINARY SEA WATER. In addition to the Brine T Massage, Electric and Vapour Baths, etc., are provided.

The Baths contain both a LADIES' and a GENT Department, and will be open during the Summer as follow

Week-days, 7·30 a.m. to 7 p.m. ; Sundays, 7·30 a.m. to 10·3

NEEDLE, VAPOUR, RUSSIAN, DOUCHE and E BATHS, as well as experienced MASSEURS, will be speciall[y] for Ladies and Gentlemen previously notifying at the Office o[r] the time at which they will be required.

————o————

SEA WATER SWIMMING BATH.

The centre of the building is occupied by a large Swimm[ing] 75 feet long and 30 feet wide, filled with tepid fresh Sea W[ater] **which Improved Heating arrangements have been i**[n] It will be open : Week-days, 7 a.m. to 8 p.m. ; Sundays, 7·3[0] 10·30 a.m. RESERVED FOR LADIES from 10 a.m. to 2 p.m. Ev[ery] EXCEPT SUNDAY.

CHARGES—

						Single Ticket.	D
SWIMMING BATH	..	..	..	..	..	1/-	
,,	after 6 p.m.	..	..	..	..	6d.	
,,	Children under 15	..	..	..	..	6d.	

SEASON TICKETS admitting to Swimming Bath any time on occasions, £1 1s. ; Children under 15 years, 10/6. Admit 6 p.m. on ordinary occasions, 10/6.

LESSONS IN SWIMMING ARE GIVEN DAILY BY EXPERIENCED ATTENDANTS.

WATER and BRINE can be had at the Baths at reasonable charges. For any further information apply to—

THE MANAGER, SALTBURN-BY-THE-SEA BRINE BATHS CO., LD., SALTBURN-BY-THE

The imposing structure of Saltburn Brine Baths built, at a cost of £6,000, in Station Square, *c.* 1890. Sadly, the baths were demolished in 1977.

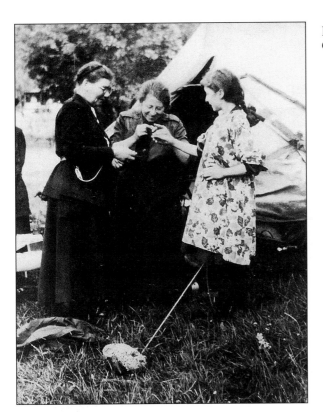

First aid at the Saltburn Girl Guides Camp, Ruswarp in 1924.

Saltburn Guides and Brownies with their shield, date unknown, which is resting upon the Brownies' wooden ceremonial mushroom.

Ready for home - Saltburn Guides Camp,
Ruswarp, 1924.

Girl Guides, Winnie Kembal and Frances
Hinchley, in 1921. The Guides were founded in
1910 by Lord Baden-Powell and his wife. The
Guide Promise is, 'I promise that I will do my best;
To do my duty to God, To serve the Queen and
help other people, and to keep the Guide Law.'

Heather Patrol 1st Saltburn Company were winners of the shield at the East Cleveland Girl Guides Rally July 1921. Leader P. Gibson, Second D. Dodson, with guides, M. Hick, B. Shaw, H. Bramley and F. Hinchley are seen here.

Heather Patrol 1st Saltburn Girl Guides were winners of the shield in May 1925.

The early days of motor racing on Saltburn sands. The gentleman on the platform, probably a coastguard, is using semaphore signals to communicate with Marske, two miles away. Communications were still in their infancy and it was vital to know that the coast was clear so another race could start. Officials carried telescopes so the flags could be clearly seen. Tents were used for officials and timekeepers, also for first aid, refreshments and perhaps even a tent for a band. Petrol was rarely available in pumps, it was bought by the gallon at chemists or ironmongers and known as motor spirit. The flat cart selling Giant Motor Spirit would carry petrol to service the racing cars. In July 1906 a crowd of 60,000, the largest in the history of Saltburn, assembled one day to watch an entry of 100 cars. Ten excursion trains arrived from the West Riding and the mining towns and villages of County Durham. The spectators were controlled by 120 policemen. What a wonderful day that must have been!

—— YORKSHIRE AUTOMOBILE CLUB. ——

(Affiliated to the Automobile Club of Great Britain and Ireland and the Motor Union.)

President - *THE RIGHT HON. EARL FITZWILLIAM.*

Official Programme and Souvenir

Of the SPEED TRIALS, to take place on the Sands between Saltburn and Marske, on Saturday, 14th July, 1906.

Commencing about One o'clock, as the Tide permits.

With the kind permission of Lord Zetland and the Councils of Saltburn & Redcar.

The Open Events are held under the Competition Rules of the Automobile Club of Great Britain & Ireland.

COPYRIGHT.

Published with the Authority of the Yorkshire Automobile Club by Wm. Rapp & Sons, The "Times" Office and Library, Saltburn, and Printed by Wm. Dresser & Sons, Darlington.

Competitors proceeded to their enclosure, at the starting point near Marske, by entering the sands at Redcar at the far end of the promenade. They made their exit by returning over the sands to Redcar, keeping as near to the sea as possible.

Officials.

Clerks of the Course—
The Committee of the Yorkshire Automobile Club and the Saltburn Committee
(Red Rosette). (White Rosette).

Judges (Badge: White and Gilt Letters)—
Messrs. J. Constantine, W. Penrose-Green, E. Gordon Learoyd, G. Scoby-Smith, Dr. Crossley Wright,

Marshal in Chief (Badge: Red Centre, White Outer Ring, Gilt Letters)—
Mr. E. H. Hepper.

Assistant Marshals (Badge: Red and Gilt Letters)—
Messrs. A. Exley, L. Hey, A. W. Dougill, E. Faiers, H. A. Jones, A. E. Masser, H. Tomlinson.

Timekeepers (Badge: Blue and Gilt Letters)—
Messrs. A. Fattorini, J. Hyland, J. E. Rhodes, J. A. Walker.

Starter (Badge: Pink and Gilt Letters)—Mr. J. Brogden.

Handicappers—The Committee of the Yorkshire Automobile Club.

Clerk of the Scales (Badge: Orange and Gilt Letters)—Mr. Charles P. Wilson.

Hon. Secretary of the Meeting (Badge: Orange and Gilt Letters)—
Mr. Charles P. Wilson, Town Hall Chambers, Leeds. Also on July 13th and 14th, Alexandra Hotel, Saltburn.

Timekeeper Antonio Fattorini owned a jewellers shop in Harrogate and he often stayed at a chalet in front of the Ship Inn, Saltburn.

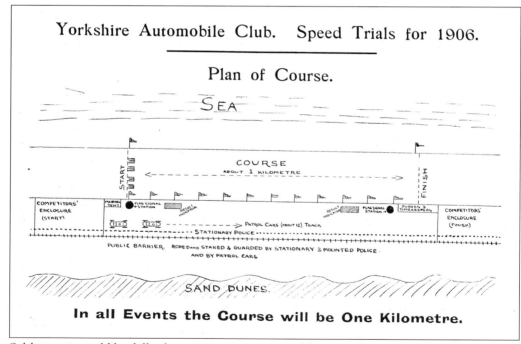

Yorkshire Automobile Club.   Speed Trials for 1906.

Plan of Course.

SEA

COURSE
ABOUT 1 KILOMETRE

START

FINISH

COMPETITORS' ENCLOSURE (START)

MARSHAL TENT

FLAG SIGNAL STATION

RESULT INDICATOR

RESULT INDICATOR

FLAG SIGNAL STATION

JUDGES & TIMEKEEPERS

COMPETITORS' ENCLOSURE (FINISH)

PATROL CARS (ABOUT 12) TRACK

STATIONARY POLICE

PUBLIC BARRIER. ROPE AND STAKED & GUARDED BY STATIONARY & MOUNTED POLICE.
AND BY PATROL CARS

SAND DUNES.

In all Events the Course will be One Kilometre.

Saltburn - it would be difficult to imagine a more suitable place of meeting than that chosen by the Yorkshire Automobile Club for the speed trials of 1906. Endowed with 10 miles of firm sands bounded on one side by steep banks, nature had outclassed the artifice of man in providing a course which delighted performers and spectators alike. This is an extract from a 1906 car racing programme.

⤜⧽ Programme of Events. ⧼⤛

EVENTS A, B, C, D, E, G, H, and I are Closed Competitions, open only to members of the Yorkshire Automobile Club and its affiliated branches.

Event A.—Closed Competition for Single Cylinder Touring Cars up to 6 h.p., carrying 2 passengers; above 6 h.p., carrying 4 passengers. **Not to exceed 8 h.p.**

To be run in heats from a standing start.   Winners of each heat to compete in the final.

1st Prize—The Club's 18 Carat Gold Medal and the "WHITEMAN" TROPHY. Presented by F. W. WOOD, Esq., of Leeds, for annual competition.

The Trophy to become the property of any competitor winning it three times in succession.
Present Holder: ALF. MASSER, Esq.

2nd Prize—The Club's 9 Carat Gold Medal.

		Name of Entrant.			Car					Driver
HEAT 1.—	1.	W. W. Stainthorpe	..	..	6 h.p. De Dion	..	..	..	..	W. Garbutt.
	2.	Guy Barrett	..	..	6 h.p. De Dion	..	..	..	..	Guy Barrett
	3.	W. Ashford	..	..	8 h.p. Cadillac	..	..	..	..	W. Robertshaw
	4.	A. L. Rhodes	..	..	6 h.p. De Dion	..	..	..	..	A. L. Rhodes

Winner.....................

HEAT 2.—	5.	F. Burr	..	..	8 h.p. Darracy	..	..	..	..	F. Burr
	6.	Alf Masser	..	..	6 h.p. De Dion	..	..	..	..	Alf. Masser
	7.	W. Robertshaw	..	..	8 h.p. Cadillac	..	..	..	..	W. Ashford

Winner.....................

Final—1st.......................   2nd.......................

Dr W.W. Stainthorpe and his 6 horsepower *De Dion* are competitors in Event A. His driver was W. Garbutt.

Saltburn Motor Races were first held for cars of all classes c. 1904. They were received with great enthusiasm by residents and visitors who crowded along the bank sides to watch. Motor racing became an annual event until the outbreak of the First World War. The races were reinstated after the war. Malcolm Campbell unofficially broke the land speed record here, in an 18 litre Sunbeam, in 1924. As the condition of the beach deteriorated cars and also motor cycles were only allowed to race for a few years more.

Event H.—Closed Competition for Touring Cars carrying 4 passengers, the chassis price of which does not exceed £600.

To be run in heats from a standing start. Winner of each heat to compete in final.

1st Prize—The Club's 18 Carat Gold Medal. 2nd Prize—The Club's 9 Carat Gold Medal.

		Name of Entrant.				Car.					Driver.
HEAT 1.—	1.	P. Graham	..	..	..	16 h.p. Rover	..	..	..	..	P. Graham
	2.	P. Fawcett	..	..	..	16 h.p. Fraschini	..	..	..	..	P. Fawcett
	3.	T. H. Woollen	..	..	..	20 h.p. Clement-Talbot	..	..	..	O. O'Grogan
	4.	C. Leather	..	..	..	16 h.p. Humber	..	..	..	..	C. Leather
	Winner........										
HEAT 2.—	5.	W. J. Wright	..	..	..	30 h.p. Darracq	..	..	..	..	W. J. Wright
	6.	K. T. W. Leather	..	..	..	18 h.p. Siddeley	..	..	..	..	K. T. W. Leather
	7.	A. Rawlinson	..	..	..	20 h.p. Darracq	..	..	..	..	S. Girling
	Winner......................										
HEAT 3.—	8.	S. S. Dixon	..	..	..	20 h.p. Darracq	..	..	..	..	S. S. Dixon
	9.	W. R. Ledgard	..	..	..	28 h.p. Mass	..	..	..	..	W. R. Ledgard
	10.	G. H. Woods	..	..	..	26 h.p. Simms Welbeck	..	..	..	..	G. H. Woods
	Winner......................										

Final—1st...................... 2nd......................

Every competitor carried numbers on the right side and back of his vehicle. The numbers were obtained at the Marshal's office, at the Competitors Enclosure, on production of the entry fee and, in the Racing Car Class, the weight certificate also.

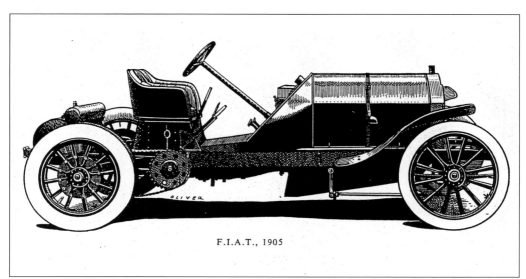

F.I.A.T., 1905

Early FIAT racing car, 1905.

Five
Entertainment

A scene from *Wishing Well*, performed by the Saltburn 53 Society. Mrs Veronica Twidle is bottom left with Dennis Greenhow, Marjorie Holmes, Alan Bewick and Prudence Rowe.

Family friends took Tom Gladders to visit Sir Alan Cobham`s Flying Circus, at Tofts Farm, in 1934.

The planes performed stunts and aerobatics and there was wing walking. Also on display was the auto-giro, forerunner of the helicopter. Meccano brought out sets of Dinky toy planes.

La Taggart, or La Taggarty as he was called by children, was a baritone singer who boasted he could also sing tenor and imitate the famous singer John McCormack. This publicity photograph was taken in the 1920s when it was said that he was a popular Dandini from the Shakespeare Theatre Programme.

In later years La Taggart (who claimed to be Italian) sang in Jack Graffo's Pierrot shows on the Bottom Promenade, in the summer. He also played piano and sang in clubs (mainly Milton Street) and pubs in winter. He is pictured wearing a Pierrot costume in the 1930s.

Renee Stonehouse (stage name Renee Valentine) was 14 years old, in 1946, when she joined the travelling theatre company of Ernie Payne and Sid Grace for two summer seasons at Saltburn Pier Theatre. It was a small company of eight to ten people so everyone had to be versatile. Ernie was a comedian and Sid was his straight man, who also played the accordion. Eddie Pullen was an acrobat and Renee was a soubrette, she sang and danced, her speciality being a tap dance on her toes wearing ballet shoes fitted with taps. Her costume was often a red and white, polka dot skirt and bodice with white muslin sleeves. The theatre and dressing rooms were on the right hand side of the pier and there was a café on the left. Every afternoon the company performed at the open air theatre, near the Hazel Grove end of Saltburn, where the audience sat on the bank side to watch. Evening shows were always at the pier. Holidays at home, after the war, meant many more people visited the seaside, guaranteeing a full house for every performance.

Veronica Twidle (right) with Sid Grace and Pat Drury. Pat was a child dancer at the Pier Theatre (often known as the Little Theatre) when Sid was performing with Eddie Payne and Company. The BBC broadcast part of Sid and Ernies pier show, live, between 1946 and 1947.

Eric Porter and George A. Cooper perform in a Shakespearean snippet for Theatre Workshop at the Spa, Saltburn. Joan Littlewood was the producer for this clever repertory company who worked without scenery, using only lighting and props for effect.

These enchanting children have been reciting nursery rhymes at a concert. *Jack and Jill* are on the right, *Ride a cock horse* at the front and also perhaps *Georgie Porgie* and *Little Miss Muffet*. Ronnie Hinchley is in the middle, second from the left. Please note the boys Eton collars and sailor suits and the girls *broderie anglais* dresses.

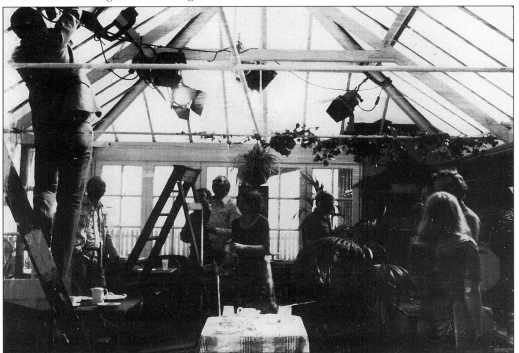

How we used to live - a documentary for Yorkshire Television filmed at the Bank Café, Saltburn, in 1975.

The Victorian Society Christmas party, 1990s. Veronica Twidle has filled many roles in Saltburn, professional actress, musician, choreographer, director and producer.

The first *End of the Pier Show*, founded by Veronica Twidle, was held in conjunction with the second year of Victorian week, in 1987, and annually thereafter. Sally Lewis (left), Sue Sellars (Pierrot), and Lily Denny are seen in the early years of the show.

Pierrots in the *End of the Pier Show*: Pat Drury, Liz Chadwick, John Munro, Vicki Wells, Tony Smith, Gordon Turner, Enid and George Shaw and Lily Denny, to name a few. The original Pierrots in Saltburn in 1890s were the *Jovial Jollies* who played for several seasons on the lower promenade and at Hazel Grove. The *Jollies* would perform three shows a day, so they had to have a large variety of costumes and routines to please their audiences. The men of the troupe went round with a collecting box after each performance. Between 1951 and 1952 the last Pierrot show, *The Great Companions*, had their final season before the Little Theatre (Pier Theatre) closed.

A scene from *South Pacific* with Gordon Turner, Tony Smith and Carol Drury.

Stewart Sykes, Tony Smith, and Gordon
Turner in the *End of the Pier Show*.

Sailors, including Lesley Inganni and Lee
and Sarah Duffield, perform in the *End of
the Pier Show*.

Miss Piggy (Pat Drury) and cockerels (Tony Smith and John Munro) perform a farmyard sketch in 1992.

Four of the ten dancers in the *Sunshine Troupe*.

Betty Middleton (centre front), with the Middleton Festival Choir. The choir was formed from a nucleus of singers from the Middleton Singers, *c.* 1977. On 13 December 1997 Mrs Betty Middleton, who came to Saltburn thirty years previously, formally handed over the choir, which bears her name, to the present conductor Elizabeth Lincoln, herself a former pupil of Betty. Born in Hull, of musical parents, music has played a large part in Betty's life, she won her first prize at the age of nine. During the war Betty formed a concert party to entertain the troops as her contribution to the war effort. She was greatly in demand as a singer but decided at the age of thirty four to abandon her singing career in favour of teaching and choral work. Betty and her husband Harry moved to Saltburn in 1956 and she formed the Middleton Singers and the Middleton Festival Choir, both well known throughout the country. So great is Betty's love of singing that she infects her pupils with her own enthusiasm and many who began with her as amateurs go on to have professional careers, sometimes becoming teachers themselves.

All who come into contact with her remember her with great affection. This indomitable lady, whose only child died in infancy, has, without doubt, brought fulfillment and happiness to many children in this area. Betty used to get up at six every morning to bake cakes to share with her pupils. Now in her eighties, but still with a powerful voice, she wonders if perhaps she should not have 'put all my eggs in one basket' and had other interests alongside her music. It seems certain that the power, love and courage which emanate from this frail lady, and the strength of the love which is returned to her by her extended family (her pupils), thoroughly justify her dedication to her music.

Betty Middleton with some of her trophies, c. 1980.

Six
Victorian Week

Sharon Wilson, Town Crier, during
Victorian Week in Saltburn.

Queen Victoria (Alice de Bonas de Mellet) with some of the Northdrifts children, Victorian Week, 1990. Saltburn's last annual Victorian Week was held in 1995, after eleven years, to be replaced by Heritage Celebrations in 1996.

An organ plays on the promenade during Saltburn Victorian Week.

Geraldine and Frank Jordan (chairman of the Victorian Society) and son during Victorian Week of 1989.

June (left) and Kath (right) take the air with a friend.

A pretty girl, spotted during Victorian Week.

Mrs Jean and the late Mr Klaus De Jong take part in Victorian Week. Jean is a well known Saltburn pianist and organist.

The Royal Signals Band played at Saltburn Victorian Week in 1989.

Brockley Hall, Victorian week, 1993. Mrs Audrey Boagey wears the Victorian costume which she created from the valances of heavy silk curtains found in the cellar of the Zetland Hotel.

Mounted police lead this Pipe
Band in Victorian Week, 1994.

Man the rigging, hoist up the
mainsail. Naval cadets visit
Saltburn during Victorian Week.

Mrs Edna Gosnay and Debbie Christon, Victorian week, probably in 1986.

Saltburn Victorians, 1992.

Saltburn's steam tradition is upheld in Victorian Week, 1989.

Leslie Crowther came to Saltburn in Victorian Week of 1990. He is seen here at Rushpool Hall.

Victorian 500 Club Wash Day. From left to right: Kath Conroy, Norman Shadlock, June Ringger, Gladys Shotton and Miss Smith.

Victorian washday. 500 Club members, Kath Conroy and June Ringger, dance in the middle.

Mrs Norwood is the lady in crinoline, 1989.

Victorians assembled outside Saltburn Railway Station.

110

Audrey Boagey and children, making gruel.

Washday! The 500 Club are busy during
Victorian Week.

Miss Jackie Taylor with her niece Ellen.

Seven
Old Saltburn

Bryan Wood 1797 - 1884.

Old Saltburn Mill, *c.* 1870, before the ironstone miners bridge was built. The mill stands on Saltburn Gill which runs into Saltburn Beck and then into the sea.

The Wood family are linked, through the years, to Old Saltburn Mill. Robert Wood (born 1753) had nine children. The first, Thomas, was born at Kilton Mill, where Robert was miller, and the rest at Saltburn Mill where he and his wife Mary (Crossley) moved after one year. Saltburn Mill was leased (as was Kilton) from John Hall Stevenson of Skelton. The rent at Saltburn was £4 10s 6d, twice a year. Robert died in 1800, aged 47 years, leaving 'goods to the value of £100' to Mary in his will.

Mary carried on at the mill, first with the help of eldest son Thomas, and later with Robert, her third son. By the 1841 census the mill was being run by Robert and Bryan (sixth son) Wood. In 1851 Robert retired and Bryan, aged 54, took over the mill with the help of his two sons, Robert and Thomas. Robert stayed on at the mill with parents Bryan and Mary (Danley) and married Elizabeth Thubron, of Hob Hill farm, in 1869. Bryan and Mary retired to 20 Ruby Street, leaving the mill in the hands of Robert and Elizabeth.

Copy of obituary.

The North Eastern Evening Gazette
Wednesday, August 6th, 1884.

Death of old residents at Saltburn

"There have passed away within a week two of the oldest residents of Saltburn. Mr Bryan Wood died last Wednesday & his wife on Tuesday morning closed her earthly career. Both were in their 86th year and saw Saltburn in its smuggling days. Mr. & Mrs Wood were beloved by all who knew them. Although the end was but natural at such an age, there is a feeling of regret in Saltburn that the last link which bound the past to the present has finally snapped"

Ship Inn and Old Saltburn, 1898. It is worth noting that when Robert Wood died in 1800 he left only 'Goods to the value of £100'. When Bryan and Mary died in 1884 Bryan left £3,291 and had also earlier obtained the milling rights which were left to his son Robert. When the mill was dismantled a secret chamber, near the waterwheel, was found. It is said that 'On one occasion a Preventative Officer was almost drowned when the race was turned on while he was inspecting the waterwheel' and 'An old lady sat on a keg of gin and hid it beneath her voluminous skirts.' Perhaps Bryan (and Robert) augmented their income by providing a safe house for John Andrews' smugglers booty. We shall never know!

The miners timber footbridge and Saltburn Mill with Cat Nab and the Ship Inn visible in the distance. The mill had become inefficient by 1902, after the advent of the powerful steam driven mills at Yarm, and was demolished in 1905. The footbridge was pulled down in 1906 after the mines closed.

Old Saltburn, 1904. The following unique extracts of life centred around the Ship Inn and Old Saltburn are taken from the memoirs of Mrs Frances Alma Addison (née Shepherd), written in 1993 when she was eighty-eight years of age.

SALTBURN AND HUNT CLIFF, SALTBURN-BY-THE-SEA

'I was Alma Shepherd born 25 September 1905, grand daughter of Robert and Ellen Welsh, better known in their early days as 'Boss' and 'Gold' as Boss was very easy going and Ellen had very golden hair and had won a large gold medal for cycling,. After an illness Boss was to rest and my grandmother, who was a very determined woman, took him to Saltburn to live in the cottage at the other end of the Ship Inn row. They took over the Ship Inn when it became vacant and they lived there for the rest of their lives.'

We see here the Ship Inn and cottages after Boss built two holiday chalets on the land at the front. Gold had green fingers and created a garden all around the Ship. Miss Oakley lived in the cottage next door, next were the Woods, third John King and on the end Miss Gladys Walton of Rushpool Hall, who had taken the cottage after Boss and Gold Welsh moved into the Ship. There were more chalets around the side and rear of the Ship.

A view, from Hunt Cliff, of the rear of the Ship Inn with chalets surrounded by gardens, *c.* 1920s. There were countless bathing machines, to quote Alma, 'Horses pulled Woodrows bathing machines to the sea and out would come some very strange customers, in bathing costumes which must have been stored for years. They had short sleeves and were down to the ankles. Some of the ladies looked hilarious to the spectators and were christened Cannon Street Angels! They were not ladylike when told that only men could enter the Ship and the women could have a drink in the garden.'

Boss and Gold had five children, this is their daughter Almina who married Dave Mulholland.

'Rent Dinner Day was hectic. Lord Zetland's agent came to collect the rent for the farms, then they partook of a wonderful dinner. I have a photo of Mr Fordham, the agent, with my grandfather Boss sitting in the front garden of the Ship Inn.' The picture mentioned is shown here, Mr Fordham is on the left.

Daughter Anne, *c.* 1885, who married Bob Johnson.

Daughter Beatrice, here in costume, became an opera singer and sang at the Albert Hall. She married Mr Reginald Harkness.

Newly weds Beatrice and Reg Harkness, who was serving with the Royal Artillery Regiment, in the First World War, at that time. To quote Alma, 'At that time soldiers were billeted in huts built on the back garden of the Ship Inn. The far kitchen (above the stables) underwent changes as the army took it over. We had the one downstairs, which had a hot air oven and fortunately a big larder, leading off the room which had wooden shutters and was quite cosy and quiet. An enormous army range was put in the far kitchen. At that time the army commandeered the haystacks from the two fields going to Brotton which belonged to the Ship. We went to the woods to gather bracken for hens and pigs bedding and how we loved it, and dropped the lot we had gathered, when the church bells started ringing on 11 November. We ran back to the Ship where all the beer was given away and we got lemonade, as much as we wanted, and cake and biscuits kept in readiness by grandma. She was very interested in war news, possibly having had for her father a colour sergeant in the Crimea, and had grown into a very correct and regimental person herself. She was a true worker. We were later to watch boats go out and throw flowers and wreaths on to the sea. The schoolchildren marched to the end of the pier and threw in theirs.'

Son Robert 'Bob' Welsh, who enlisted in a cavalry regiment, 1925.

Frances Catherine Shepherd (née Welsh) was the daughter of Boss and Gold and the mother of Mrs Frances Alma Addison, the writer of this family history. Here we see Frances Catherine with a group of holidaymakers outside the Ship in the 1940s.

Private James Shepherd served as a clerk to War Graves in France in the First World War. He also served commendably in the Second World War.

Boss with Almina and her husband and their daughter Jean.

A delightful portrait of Almina (left) and Anne Welsh.

Frances Catherine Welsh on board a ship which crashed through the pier in 1924. Alma wrote, 'Two ships ran ashore on the rocks and my brother became friendly with both captains. We were at Thornaby and the ships came every month to the flour mill on the Tees, my brothers grew interested in ships and both became merchant ship captains.' The Ship took in shipwrecked sailors and they were cared for there. Ellen 'Gold' Welsh laid out seamen's bodies in the tiny mortuary nearby.

Charabanc outing. At the bottom left is Dave Mulholland, third along from the left is Frances Alma Shepherd. Alma takes up the story, 'After the war had finished charabancs became popular. I remember several trips to Whitby, from Watson's garage near the Zetland Hotel, with a box of chocolates from Boss, from Ainsley's cake shop. They also brought trippers from Middlesbrough and other towns'.

An outing from Saltburn, *c.* 1890. Anne Welsh sits to the left of the lady in the striped dress.

A Saltburn gathering, bottom right is Ellen 'Gold' Welsh next to Robert 'Boss' Welsh. Anne sits above Gold and Beatrice is next to the toddler.

Almina Welsh is on the end of the front row, right hand side, of this party on a trip from Saltburn.

Anne Welsh, playing with Beatrice's son, in a beached fishing boat.

Anti-tank traps outside the Ship Inn, during the Second World War. 'My grandmother Gold Welsh continued to run the Ship Inn, for many years, after my grandfather's death. When she died (around 1945) my uncle Bob continued. So I think Welshes must have had it for sixty years.'

In the 1940s the chalets on the front disappeared into the sea, but let us end this story where we began, in Old Saltburn. This view of the back of the Ship Inn shows Gold in her garden and Boss leaning on the fence talking to a friend. The last word is from Alma, 'Apart from the sale of beer and spirits there was a great demand for ham (home cured), cheese or crab sandwiches, also fat rascals which my grandma kept on making and my family still demand'.